DEVOTIONAL OUTLINES ON THE TABERNACLE

by

Glenn M. Jones

KREGEL PUBLICATIONS
Grand Rapids, Michigan

Devotional Outlines on the Tabernacle, by Glenn M. Jones. © 1987 by Glenn M. Jones. Thoroughly revised, updated, and published by Kregel Publications, a division of Kregel, Inc. P. O. Box 2607, Grand Rapids, MI 49501. All rights reserved.

Library of Congress Cataloging-in-Publication Data

Jones, Glenn M.
  [Big ten tabernacle topics]
  Devotional outlines on the tabernacle / Glenn M. Jones.
        p.   cm.
  Reprint. Originally published: Big ten tabernacle topics.
Chicago: Moody Press, 1959.

  1. Tabernacle—Typology—Outlines, syllabi, etc. 2. Typology (Theology)—Outlines, syllabi, etc. I. Title.
BS680.T32J66   1989   220.6'4—dc19   88-22759
                                                  CIP

  ISBN   0-8254-2966-8 (pbk.)

1 2 3 4 5 Printing/Year 93 92 91 90 89

Printed in the United States of America

CONTENTS

USE OF THE ILLUSTRATIONS

The following carefully prepared outlines are designed for use with the illustrations on pages 67-70. These should be referred to frequently during your study. You may wish to color the drawings which will improve their attractiveness and effectiveness. Applying the colors indicated in Exodus chapters 35-39 will also impress upon your mind more vividly the symbolism of these colors.

A large teaching chart containing these illustrations is available. Request a free sample with coloring instructions from the author: G. M. Jones, 1003 Lake Ave., Prudenville, MI 48651.

USE OF THE OUTLINES

The ten outlines contained herein briefly cover our subject, "The Tabernacle in the Wilderness," including an outline on the high priestly apparel. While it is not our intent to cover every facet of this inexhaustible subject, a considerable amount of material may be found within these pages. Many good volumes have already been written. Among the best, we believe, are *The Tabernacle in the Wilderness* by I. M. Haldeman and two excellent studies by H. W. Soltau: *Holy Vessels and Furniture of the Tabernacle* and *The Tabernacle, The Priesthood, and The Offerings.*

The following outlines are recommended for use as lecture or sermon material in connection with the illustrations already discussed. This material will give you the key—significant truth relevant to the various phases of this study. It is important to seek the guidance of the Holy Spirit in addition to making yourself extremely well-acquainted with this great subject. Reference material is readily available from your local Christian bookstore, or from the publisher of these outlines.

FOREWORD

The author readily recognizes the excellent treatment already given by many to this fascinating and important subject, "The Tabernacle in the Wilderness."

It is our purpose to provide, by summarizing and making available in outline form, both old and new material relevant to this subject. Condensed data in readily usable form which is based on these divinely inspired truths should prove to be an asset to Bible teachers, preachers, and students.

One of the most important prerequisites and a basic premise to a proper understanding of this subject is a divine consciousness of the fact that the Mosaic Law never did, never can, or never will save one human soul. The Mosaic Law of God is so infinitely perfect that it condemns the human soul. It is a fact also, as the Bible clearly teaches, that all the blood sacrifices offered by Israel as part of the tabernacle worship were only expressions of faith in God's way of salvation. The exercise of this personal faith in God resulted in the postponement of divine judgment upon sin until, in the divine plan of God, Christ should come and cancel this sin debt. On this basic premise, humankind can now be reconciled to God. Salvation was, and always will be, by the grace of God through faith in the Lord Jesus Christ.

Perhaps you have asked the question, "Why study the tabernacle in the wilderness?" The answer is found in the Bible itself. First of all, the tabernacle and the tabernacle form of worship are figures of that which was to come (Heb. 9:8, 9, 24). It was a shadow or profile of God's future plans (Heb. 10:1). The tabernacle and the tabernacle form of worship were examples and a pattern established by God for the benefit of those in the ages to come (1 Cor. 10:11; Heb. 8:5).

Furthermore, we read in the Gospels that He began with Moses and the Prophets to teach them out of their Law (Luke 24:27). Jesus Himself admonishes us to "search the scriptures; for in them ye think ye have eternal life: and *they are they which testify of me*" (John 5:39). The Scriptures to which our Lord refers certainly included the Law and the Prophets; these were in existence during the time of Christ's earthly ministry. According to His own words, our Savior must have taught concerning the tabernacle in the wilderness.

The theme of the tabernacle in the wilderness is the blood. This, in fact, is the central theme of the Word of God, as it relates to the finished work of the Son of God. In Leviticus 17:11 we read: "For it is the blood that maketh an atonement for the soul." Also, the inspired writer to the Hebrews expresses the importance of the blood in relation to the salvation of the human soul, for we read: "And without shedding of blood [there] is no remission" (Heb. 9:22).

The principal act in the tabernacle form of worship was the slaying of the sacrifical lamb or other blood sacrifices as required by the law. We sincerely believe, due to the importance that the Holy Scriptures place upon tabernacle life as it related to the children of Israel, that these sacrifices can represent nothing less than a shadow and a pattern of things to come and is every bit typical of the fact that "the blood of Jesus Christ his Son cleanseth us from all sin" (1 John 1:7).

As you peruse these pages, keep in mind our Lord's admonition to "search the scriptures: for in them ye think ye have eternal life: and *they are they which testify of me*." We trust that our great Lord and Savior Jesus Christ, through the divine operation of the Spirit of God, will enrich your service for Him, as you proceed to examine this work and utilize its content.

Outline 1

INTRODUCTION AND THE OUTER COURT

I. BACKGROUND INFORMATION
    A. Exodus 25:1-9; Hebrews 9
    B. Order of Events Leading to the Divine Command
        to Build the Tabernacle
    C. General Data of Interest Concerning the
        Illustrations

II. THE OUTER COURT (Exodus 27:9-19)
    A. Size: 150 feet by 75 feet by 7 $\frac{1}{2}$ feet high
    B. Materials
        1. Fine Linen (Revelation 19:8)
        2. Silver
        3. Brass and Wood
    C. The Gate (Exodus 27:16)
        1. Size: 30 feet wide by 7 $\frac{1}{2}$ feet high
        2. Colors: Blue, Purple, Scarlet, and White
        3. The Four Pillars
        4. The Way (John 14:6; Acts 4:12)

I. BACKGROUND INFORMATION

A. Exodus 25:1-9; Hebrews 9
B. Order of Events Leading to the Divine Command to Build the Tabernacle

After reading the Scripture references and summarizing, in story form, the events leading to the initiation of the tabernacle plan, reflect on why we believe God revealed His plan to

Moses beginning with the innermost part—the Ark of the Covenant (Exodus 25:10). There is a divine principle here. God always begins with the heart and works outward.

Our redemption was wrought in this manner. It began in love, dear to the heart of God, and it begins in our hearts today when we place our implicit trust in Him as our personal Savior. Man begins on the outside and tries to work his way in. Especially is this true in respect to man's inherent tendency to work for his own salvation. Human nature has not changed since the days of Cain. We are still prone to present our own offering of human efforts to the Lord, rather than accept His love offering—the Lord Jesus Christ, the Lamb of God, slain before the foundation of the world.

The ark of the covenant, as we will find later, represents the very throne of God. Our studies begin with the way in; that is, through the gate to the sacrificial Lamb. Like Christian in *Pilgrim's Progress,* we progress through life in adoration, service, and worship, until we reach heaven itself, but first, we must approach the Lamb of God for salvation. We must accept God's provision and place our implicit trust in Jesus Christ for salvation.

The Holy of Holies in the tabernacle represents heaven itself. Our approach, then, to this subject—the tabernacle in the wilderness—will represent the way God has ordained that man should approach Him. We do not begin our study with the ark of the covenant, but we begin with the gate, or the way in. Jesus said: "I am the way, the truth, and the life," so we begin with Him—as the Way. Our salvation begins with Him. Unless we recognize this first of all, we shall never reach that celestial place in His eternal presence.

C. General Data of Interest Concerning the Tabernacle Illustrations

In focusing your attention on the illustrations (pp. 67-70), be certain to reiterate and re-focus on the theme of its message: "The Blood That Maketh an Atonement for the Soul." By way of passing interest, the scale used in the design of this drawing is 18 inches representing 1 cubit. Exodus gives these dimensions in cubits. The illustration has been designed to this scale, as far as it is possible to do so.

The Scriptures do not indicate the dimensions for the laver or the candlestick. We believe the Holy Spirit has reasons for this, which will be revealed later in our studies. The Holy Spirit was very careful to reveal to Moses His exact plan for the tabernacle. This He did down to the very minutest detail. The drawing reveals much of this detail. Every line on the illustrations conforms, as far as we believe it is humanly possible, to the biblical account.

Notice the enlarged arrangement of the tabernacle furniture on page 67. This falls into the shape of a cross. The location of this furniture is not coincidental, but exactly as God revealed it to Moses in the Book of Exodus.

Permit me to emphasize, once again, the words of our Savior: "Search the scriptures . . . they are they which testify of me" (John 5:39). We sincerely believe this study testifies of Jesus Christ and His finished work. If this is true, then we must believe also that somewhere within this glorious revelation of Himself, we will find the Church—the bride of Christ. The typical truth revealed in our study is predicated on the fact that the tabernacle in the wilderness is a picture of our Lord, His finished work on the Cross, and the results of that finished work.

II. THE OUTER COURT (Exodus 27:9-19)

A. Size: 150 feet by 75 feet by 7 $\frac{1}{2}$ feet high

These dimensions, as previously stated, represent 18 inches for every cubit of measure indicated in Exodus 27:9-19. The cost of the tabernacle, including the outer court, the brazen altar, and laver has been estimated at $1,500,000, based on pre-inflation values. All of this equipment was portable. Today we would call such an edifice "prefabricated construction".

B. Materials

The materials used for the outer court, as well as for the entire tabernacle, provide a very interesting study, to say the least. There is a preponderance of information relevant to the symbolical teaching ascribed to these materials and colors. We will merely summarize that which is generally accepted typical teaching.

1. Fine Linen (Revelation 19:8)

The outer court fabric was a fine linen material. We find the fine linen in Revelation 19:8 representing the righteousness of the bride or church of Jesus Christ. We know that our righteousness is none other than Christ Himself (1 Cor. 1:30; 2 Cor. 5:21). The linen, therefore, for the outer court represents Jesus Christ in all His purity and absolute righteousness.

Yet this picture of our Lord extends even further. This linen was made from flax, and flax is grown from the ground. Here we have a beautiful picture of His sinless humanity and His earthly ministry—the One who became part of this world that He might bring us to God. Here we have the One who knew no sin, but became sin for us (see 2 Cor. 5:21).

The outer court kept all that was defiled away from God's place of worship. The first act of worship was through the court gate to the place of blood sacrifice. No member of the human race today can worship God except through the provision God Himself has made—the sacrifice of His own Son. The outer court also speaks of protection, inasmuch as it enclosed those who came to God with their offerings.

2. Silver

The pillars, capped with silver, held the linen sheet in place, and exposed the linen for all to see. Herein lies a precious truth for us today. These pillars may well represent believers in Christ holding up, for the world to see, the righteousness of God which is Jesus Christ.

Let us look at this picture more closely. What do we find, relative to these many pillars, that cause us to believe these represent the believer? Silver in the Word of God invariably speaks of redemption.

To begin with, all the material for the tabernacle was given as a freewill offering, except the silver. The same amount of silver was required of each Israelite for the tabernacle. Our redemption cost something and the price is the same for every member of the human race. The cost was the precious blood of the Son of God, and whether we are rich or poor, male or female, bond or free, we must all come by the way of the cross for salvation.

During the days of the Israelites, slaves were bought with silver. You and I were purchased out of the slave market of sin with the redemptive power of the blood of Christ. You will remember how Joseph was sold for silver; also our Lord was sold for silver by Judas. Our redemption cost God all that He had. The hymn writer wrote: "Jesus paid it all, all to Him I owe; sin had left a crimson stain, He washed it white as snow."

3.   Brass and Wood

The pillars were made of brass. The Scriptures are not too clear whether these were solid brass or shittim wood overlaid with brass. These pillars were at least 7 $\frac{1}{2}$ feet high. Portability was an important factor in the overall construction. Perhaps solid brass pillars would have been excessively heavy.

It appears to me that shittim wood, sometimes called acacia wood, must have been used also. In any event, we shall see later how shittim wood is a picture of humanity, and, if this is true, these pillars again speak of the believer here on earth.

Brass is a picture of divine judgment. This is unmistakably true, especially as we see this material in use elsewhere throughout the tabernacle. You will remember the brazen serpent held on a pole in the wilderness, and how all those who would look upon this serpent would live. This certainly was a picture of our Lord bearing our judgment on the tree. Jesus Himself alluded to this when He talked to Nicodemus, for He said: "As Moses lifted up the serpent in the wilderness, even so must the Son of man be lifted up" (John 3:14). The pillars of brass were seated on plates of brass, speaking, we believe, of judgment underneath.

By way of summary, we now have a picture of a believer who has been crowned with redemption, and, although condemned to die, one who now has the judgment of God under his feet. In addition to this, we now find him holding up to a dying world the divine righteousness of God.

C. The Gate (Exodus 27:16)

Let us approach the grand climax to our lesson—the gate, or way, to the brazen altar.

1. Size: 30 feet wide by 7 $\frac{1}{2}$ feet high

Notice, the gate was 30 feet wide. The court gate was the only way in. Christ, who said, "I am the way" (John 14:6), is our only way into right relationship with God. The wide gate is a picture of the easy and simple way of salvation offered to all.

2. Colors: Blue, Purple, Scarlet, and White

The gate was similar to the court itself, except that colors were woven into the linen. These colors were blue, purple, scarlet, and white (permit us to call white a color). Why these particular colors? Certainly the Holy Spirit did not choose these at random. May we suggest that each of these colors has a significant typical teaching. If the linen speaks of Christ's righteousness, then we believe that these colors must speak also of Him. This is especially true when we realize that these colors are found nowhere else in the outer court, but in the gateway only.

In harmony with what we are about to say, let us be reminded, first, of the four Gospels—Matthew, Mark, Luke, and John. You will recall that Matthew portrays our Lord as the King of the Jews. This Gospel is sometimes called the Kingdom Gospel. The Gospel of Mark pictures Christ as the Servant, obedient even unto death, while Luke depicts Him as the Son of man. The Gospel of John portrays our Lord as the Son of God.

With these facts relative to the Gospels established in our minds, let us take a careful look at the colors woven into the linen gate curtains. The blue may well represent Christ as the heavenly one, as we find Him in the Gospel of John, the Son of God. The purple, which was and is even today the color of royalty, may represent, in type, our Lord as King—the Son of David, as we find Him in the Gospel of Matthew. The scarlet, color of blood or sacrifice, certainly pictures for us the Lord Jesus Christ as we find Him in the Gospel of Mark—the Servant obedient unto death. White is the color which represents purity or righteousness. We find our Lord as the Son of man in the Gospel of Luke—the Holy One, the Sinless One. These colors, as we find them here in the gate or elsewhere in the tabernacle, represent, we believe, the Lord Jesus in this marvelous fourfold sense.

We would like to mention another interesting item. The gate curtains did not contain the interwoven cherubim. Later, we shall find the cherubim intricately woven into the inner veil. Cherubim, we shall find, speak of guardians of His holiness. No guards were needed at the gate, for the gate was the entrance to "whosoever will may come." God has placed no barriers to anyone who will come to His Lamb for salvation.

3.　The Four Pillars

We have seen how the linen gate, with its colors, speaks to us of Christ. Does it seem illogical to assume that the four pillars, which support the gate curtains, speak to us of the four writers of the Gospels? We have already noted how the outer court pillars can represent every believer in Christ. The Word of God does not indicate that the gate pillars were any different than the many other outer pillars. Certainly the writers of the

Gospels were sinners saved by the grace of God, the same as you and I.

4. The Way (John 14:6; Acts 4:12)

We have spoken concerning the gate as the way, and representing Christ who said, "I am the way, the truth, and the life: no man cometh unto the Father, but by me." I suggest that you conclude this section focusing on its evangelistic emphasis, carefully studying the great truths found in John 14:6 and Acts 4:12.

You may wish to survey the high points in this outline very briefly before concluding. A vivid investigation of the crucifixion of God's sacrificial Lamb, along with appropriate personal application, is certainly in order. This will reaffirm these truths in your heart and mind.

As Bezaleel was filled with the Spirit of God (Exodus 35:30-35) and directed by the Holy Spirit to construct the tabernacle, so it is essential that we be filled with the Holy Spirit as we study the Word of God and teach it to others.

Outline 2

THE BRAZEN ALTAR AND LAVER

I. THE BRAZEN ALTAR OF BURNT OFFERING (Exodus
   27:1-8; 30:17-21)
   A. Size: 7 $\frac{1}{2}$ feet by 7 $\frac{1}{2}$ feet by 4 $\frac{1}{2}$ feet high
   B. Materials: Shittim Wood, Brass, and Horns
   C. The Lamb and Fire
II. THE LAVER
   A. Material: Brass (size not given)
   B. The Water (type of God's Word)

When we think of an altar, we immediately think of worship. An altar is a place of humiliation, a place of submission to something or someone. This is what happens when we come to Christ for salvation. We realize that we are sinners and accept God's sacrificial Lamb for our salvation. Following this experience, we hunger for spiritual food — God's Holy Word.

Immediately after the priests offered the sacrifice on the brazen altar, their next appointment was at the brazen laver. We shall see how this laver is a symbol of God's Word, our spiritual food.

I. THE BRAZEN ALTAR OF BURNT OFFERING (Exodus 27:1-8; 30:17-21)

A. Size: 7 $\frac{1}{2}$ feet by 7 $\frac{1}{2}$ feet by 4 $\frac{1}{2}$ feet high

The length and breadth of this altar was equivalent to the height of the outer court. The typical significance of the outer court has something in common with this brazen altar. We only need to remind ourselves of this Scripture: "And without the shedding of blood [there] is no remission [forgiveness]" (Heb. 9:22). In other words, without the shed blood of Christ on the cross, there is no forgiveness for you and me, who stand as the outer court pillars upholding the righteousness of Christ.

B. Materials: Shittim Wood, Brass, and Horns

The shittim wood, from which this altar was constructed, gives us a beautiful picture of Christ's humanity. Let us note, carefully, some of the characteristics of this wood.

First, shittim wood will withstand heat, being an indestructible type of ebony wood. Our Lord's body withstood the divine fire of God's judgment, a judgment which would have been ours. Because He did this for us, God will never require that His children suffer eternal judgment for sin. We read: "There is therefore now no condemnation [judgment] to them which are in Christ Jesus . . ." (Rom. 8:1).

Shittim wood was a desert shrub. This shrub possessed a long tap root, reaching down to the subterranean dampness. How well this reminds us of the prophet Isaiah when he wrote prophetically concerning our Lord's humanity, saying: ". . . as a root out of a dry ground: he hath no form nor comeliness . . . " (Isa. 53:2). The prophet, in this verse, is speaking of the humanity of Christ. The common shrub growing in that arid region was none other than the acacia tree, known as shittim wood.

We have seen from our lesson on the outer court, how brass is a symbol of divine judgment. Here again, we have the shittim wood overlaid with brass. The brazen altar was the place where the sacrificial lamb was slain, and where the body of this lamb was required to endure the altar fire. We now see how this lamb is a type of the "Lamb of God." We have, in the altar itself, a picture of the cross of Christ, where Christ bore our penalty for sin. "The Lord hath laid on him the iniquity of us all" (Isa. 53:6). Just as the brazen altar was the only place where the children of Israel could come to receive postponement of divine judgment for their sins, so the cross of Christ—the Lamb on that cross—is the only place we can approach today to receive forgiveness of sin.

We now encounter something new in our study—the horns which were placed at each corner on the top of the brazen altar. Why were they there? What was their purpose? We are not clear as to their function, but we are quite certain as to their meaning in Scripture.

These horns were found only on this altar and on the altar of incense. We believe they speak of power. Later, we shall find the altar of incense representing prayer. We know the power that is to be found in prayer, and we know the power of the blood of Christ of which the altar of burnt offering is symbolic. Often we sing the old hymn, "There Is Power in the Blood."

In addition to this, we find Daniel speaking of powers, or kings, as ten horns and one little horn, which came up after the ten horns (Dan. 7:24). All this causes us to believe the Holy Spirit would like to have us think of these horns as representing His power.

C. The Lamb and Fire

Certainly we need to read only a portion of the Epistle to the Hebrews to learn that the animal sacrifices offered on the brazen altar were a type of our Lord Jesus Christ. These sacrifices, subjected to the intense heat of the altar fire, represent our Lord being subjected to the divine judgment of God poured out upon Him on the Cross.

The judgment or condemnation that was ours, He endured for you and me. Let us notice the Scriptures that bring this marvelous truth to our attention: "Christ . . . hath given himself for us an offering and a sacrifice to God" (Eph. 5:2). "So Christ was once offered to bear the sins of many" (Heb. 9:28). "For it is not possible that the blood of bulls and of goats should take away sins" (Heb. 10:4). "Behold the Lamb of God, which taketh away the sin of the world" (John 1:29; see also 1 Peter 1:18, 19).

II. The Laver (type of God's Word)

A. Material: Brass (size not given)

We find the laver consisting of brass, but nowhere do we read concerning the size of the laver. The laver is a picture of God's Holy Word in a very real sense. The question is: *How* does the laver speak to us of God's Word, inasmuch as the laver was made of brass?

We have already seen how brass speaks of divine judgment. In Psalm 119, we find the Word of God called the judgment of God at least 15 times. Certainly when you and I read God's Word we soon find that we are being judged. To begin with, we are judged as sinners, condemned at every turn, and without Christ—eternally lost (Rom. 3; 6).

This judgment upon us is boundless. We cannot fathom the terribleness of our sin in the eyes of infinite holiness; that is, holiness absolute. This is the reason God required an infinite sacrifice to justify you and me in the eyes of an infinitely holy God. The laver was boundless, in the sense that no size or weight was given to it. We believe this vessel was comparatively small, inasmuch as it was transportable and we know the weight of brass to be even heavier than iron, depending upon its density.

The laver was made from the brass looking glasses, which were used undoubtedly by the women. We read of God's Word being associated with a looking glass (James 1:23, 24).

B. The Water

Again we find the water, in the laver, to be representative of God's Word. It was mandatory for the priest to wash at the laver before entering the tabernacle. If he should fail to wash, he would die (Exod. 30:20, 21).

Before we continue, permit me to interject this practical lesson: should you and I fail to come to God's Word regularly for cleansing, we will also die spiritually, as far as being any use to our Lord is concerned. Jesus said: "Now ye are clean though the word which I have spoken unto you" (John 15:3). The whole Bible is the Word of God, as well as the words spoken by our Lord, and we need to read and meditate upon it regularly.

Water was used as a symbol of God's Word by Jesus Himself during His discourse with Nicodemus (John 3:5). We read: "Except a man be born of water and of the Spirit, he cannot enter into the kingdom of God."

Permit me to digress somewhat here and show why I believe the water, referred to by our Lord, does not represent water baptism. Jesus is speaking of being born again, or born of God. This same terminology is used by the apostle Peter where we read: "*Being born again,* not of corruptible seed, but of incorruptible, by the *Word of God,* which liveth and abideth forever" (1 Peter 1:23).

In Paul's Epistle to the Romans, we find that we are saved by faith, and this faith is received by hearing the Word of God (Rom. 10:17). The Scripture consistently teaches that being born again, or regeneration, is the function of the Holy Spirit in cooperation with the Word of God. The Lord Jesus Himself is called the Word of God (John 1:1-14). He is the living Word which the written Word has so vividly declared. In 1 John 5:6, 7, 8 we read of water being associated with the Word in respect to our eternal redemption in Christ Jesus.

But let us turn to Ephesians 5:26 for our final substantiating evidence. Here we read concerning the Church of Jesus Christ, the born again believers: "That he might sanctify and cleanse it with the washing of water by the Word." We hardly need to proceed further. Water in the Scriptures, when used symbolically, is a type of the Word of God and not of water baptism.

Let us look at the tabernacle scene now before us. We have the priest cleansing himself from defilement at the laver, and seeing himself as he is—reflected by the water and the polished brass. This was his solemn duty before God. He was cognizant of the results if he did not wash before entering the tabernacle—God's place of worship. What a lesson for the children of God today!

Certainly you and I need to approach God's Word in an atmosphere of holy reverence. We should trust Him to show us our sin, and then cleanse ourselves from all filthiness of the flesh. For this cleansing, let us claim His promise: "If we confess our sins, he is faithful and just to forgive us our sins, and to cleanse us from all unrighteousness" (1 John 1:9).

This outline concludes with an appeal to holy living. The message of salvation is everywhere in this lesson. Only the Holy Spirit is fully able to direct you to apply properly this message.

You will readily realize that we have touched only the high points. This is in harmony with the purpose of these outlines. A preponderance of material relating to the brazen altar and the laver may be found in the Word of God and elsewhere, if we diligently seek for it.

I suggest that you refer continually to the illustrations during your study. This will help you grasp the subject matter and keep it pictorially impressed on your mind.

Outline 3

THE TABERNACLE STRUCTURE
(Exodus 26)

I.   THE BOARDS AND BARS
     A. Materials: Gold and Wood—Sockets of Silver
     B. The Bars: Gold and Wood
II. THE CURTAINS
     A. Inner or First Curtain (fine-twined linen)
     B. Second Curtain (goat's hair)
III. THE COVERINGS
     A. Rams' Skins Dyed Red (hidden from view)
     B. Badger Skins: Outer Covering (unattractive)
IV. THE DOOR
     A. The Linen
     B. The Pillars

   The tabernacle was constructed according to a divine plan in which Jehovah God was the Supreme Architect and Moses the general contractor. Moses was given many skilled workers, among whom was Bezaleel, his foreman. This man was especially endowed with the Holy Spirit. Similarly, we are workers with Christ in building His Church. Christian service is not so much working for the Lord as working with Him.

   The tabernacle structure was 45 feet long, 15 feet wide, and 15 feet high. The Holy Place was 30 feet long, and the Holy of Holies 15 feet long. The Holy of Holies constituted that area behind the veil where the ark of the covenant was placed. This room was a perfect cube, being 15 feet in all directions. By way of interest, we find the New Jerusalem to be 1,500 miles cubed (Rev. 21:16).

I. THE BOARDS AND BARS

The boards, which were assembled vertically and locked together, constituted the structural pieces of the tabernacle. These were fabricated from shittim (acacia) wood and overlaid with pure gold. The boards were seated into silver sockets.

We shall find, as we continue our study, the total absence of brass within this holy place of worship. There is no place for divine judgment here, as all was taken care of at the Cross—the brazen altar. The priest, who had also washed at the laver, is now qualified to worship God in the tabernacle. These priests represent the believer today. We remember believers are called priests in the New Testament (Rev. 1:6; 5:10). The high priest, beginning with Aaron, is in every way a type of Christ, our High Priest, who "ever liveth to make intercession for us" (Heb. 7:25).

As we approach the interior of this holy structure and notice the absence of brass, we are reminded of the absence of judgment or condemnation for the believer who has had the blood of Christ applied (the brazen altar) and has come to God's Word for cleansing (the laver).

A. Material: Gold and Wood—Sockets of Silver

We behold the wooden boards covered with gold and immediately think of our Lord, who was both human and divine. Let us see, in these boards, a picture of the believer as well. Gold is generally accepted as being a type of divinity or representative of Christ's divinity and deity. Generally speaking, authorities on Bible typology agree to this.

Some of the reasons for accepting this typical significance placed upon gold are as follows: Gold is practically indestructible and when subjected to fire becomes even more refined. Our Lord, when submitted to the judgment fire of Almighty God at Calvary's cross did not falter, but was gloriously victorious.

Furthermore, we shall find that the candlestick of beaten gold and the golden ark of the covenant definitely picture for us the Lord Jesus Christ. In Revelation 21:18 we see that the city of God is made of pure gold. These facts lead us to believe that gold is a Bible symbol of that which is divine.

The boards picture for us the believer, in the sense that there are many boards and they are interlocked with silver. Silver, as we have seen in our study of the outer court, represents the redemptive work of Christ. We, as God's children, are bound together because of Christ's redemptive work. In being bound together, our love for one another is the direct product of the bonds of Calvary.

The boards rested on sockets of silver. We are resting on His redemption provided for us. The wooden boards overlaid with gold speak to us of our humanity clothed with Christ's divinity. This divinity, of course, is now veiled, but when we see Him face to face, then, "we shall be *like Him,* for we shall see Him as He is" (1 John 3:2).

B. The Bars: Gold and Wood

Here again we have wood overlaid with gold, and we are told there were five bars for each side of the tabernacle. These bars were attached to the boards.

Do we not have here a picture of our Lord, particularly the grace of our Lord Jesus Christ binding all His children together? (We understand, from a study of the significance of numbers in the Scriptures, that five is frequently representative of the grace of God.)

II. THE CURTAINS

There were four layers of material covering the tabernacle. The two inner layers were called curtains and the two outer layers were called coverings. Let us now consider, first of all, the curtains.

A. Inner or First Curtain

The inner curtain, which was visible from the inside of the tabernacle, was made of fine-twined linen. Colors of blue, purple, and scarlet, were very cunningly, if not meticulously, woven into the linen. Interwoven, as an integral part of this curtain, we find cherubim. What does all of this mean? We believe Jehovah, the Great Designer, is showing to us, in type, a picture of our Lord. We see again His divine righteousness in the fine-twined linen, an Egyptian linen of which it has been said the world is not capable of producing today. We have again the colors representing Christ as the Son of God, as King, and as Servant of God and man. These colors are the same as we found in the outer court gate.

Why do we find cherubim woven into this curtain, whereas no cherubim appear in the outer court gate curtain? Cherubim speak of the guardians of His holiness, or his holiness vindicated. This truth is not difficult to establish when we remember that God placed cherubim at the east entrance to the Garden of Eden to guard the Tree of Life after Adam had sinned (Gen. 3:24).

The inner curtain was held together with taches, or fasteners of gold. The Scriptures are careful to tell us that this tabernacle is one tabernacle; that is, one perfect whole (Exod. 26:6). The taches of gold have their part in making this possible. The tabernacle is a picture of Christ and His bride, the Church, but in a greater sense, it is a picture of Christ the Head of the Church. The taches of gold speak of His divinity. Our worship, as was the priests' who worshiped in the tabernacle, must be entirely in Christ.

B. Second Curtain

The second curtain was one of goat's hair. We find it completely hidden from view to the priest inside the tabernacle. Let us consider, first of all, the material—goat's hair. The goat's hair depicts for us the blackness of sin—the sin of fallen mankind. The Palestinian goat was black, and still is today. The goat is invariably used in a bad sense throughout Scripture. We read concerning the separation of the sheep from the goats in respect to the good and bad nations (Matt. 25:32). Goats were used as a sin offering to God; this we find in Leviticus 16:5. This, therefore, pictures for us the blackness of sin.

Another significant observation is found in the fact that the goat's hair curtain was covered with the covering of ram's skin dyed red. This gives us a beautiful picture of the blood of Jesus Christ covering the sins of the world.

The goat's hair curtain was held together with taches of brass, telling us again of judgment associated with sin. We read in the Scriptures (Exod. 26:9, 12, 13) that the goat's hair curtain was made to hang down over the front edge of the tabernacle a distance of one cubit. This portion was exposed to the view of all Israel's encampment. Is not this a picture of the One who knew not sin, yet *became* sin for us, and ministered the short period of three years, exposed to man's insults and finally the death of the cross? Certainly to the outside world He was despised and rejected, and ultimately judged as a malefactor.

III. THE COVERINGS

The coverings were of more durable material than the curtains and provided adequate protection for the tabernacle.

A. Rams' Skins Dyed Red

The inner covering, which rested upon the goat's hair curtain, consisted of rams' skins dyed red. We have already touched upon this and sincerely believe this to represent our Lord's substitutionary death. The world does not see His death as substitutionary, neither could the world see the covering of the red rams' skins (1 Cor. 1:18). Christ's blood shelters the Christian and covers his sin; so it was with the rams' skins covering that sheltered the tabernacle and covered the goat's hair curtain.

B. Badger Skins: Outer Covering

We now come to the outer covering—that of badger skins. The color has not been revealed in the Scriptures, but it must have been unattractive to an observer on the outside. Inasmuch as the tabernacle is a picture of Christ, our salvation, we find the tabernacle appearing unattractive to the outside world. But what glories we behold directly underneath its coverings and curtains! The Lord Jesus is unattractive to the world at large, but how precious to those who love Him, and are redeemed by His blood.

The badger skin covering provided adequate protection from the worldly elements; so Christ shields His own from the onslaughts of Satan. We can sing with the poet, "He hideth my soul in the cleft of the rock, and covers me there with His hand."

IV. THE DOOR

Jesus said, "I am the door . . ." (John 10:9), and we know He is the way of life, the entrance not only to an abundant life here, but to life eternal beyond. He has been made unto us righteousness, and everything blessed that God desires for us.

We have discussed the outer court gate, the way to the Lamb offered on the altar, Christ our salvation; we have considered the laver—how we must come to God's Word after we are saved. After the priest had washed at the laver he was qualified to enter the door of the tabernacle and worship God within.

Consider, if you will, this door as the way to acceptable worship of God, the way to communion and fellowship with Him. We read John 10:7: "I am the door of *the sheep. . . .*" Jesus is telling His sheep that He is their door as well as the door for the sinner to come for salvation. It is Christ, as the believer's door, that we wish to see in the typical truth before us.

A. The Linen

The linen and colors in the door were identical to those found in the gate. This again is a picture or type of our Lord in the same manner we found in the court gate. Jesus said:

"No man cometh to the Father but by me" (John 14:6). We, as believers, must come to the Father in Jesus' name and through Him, who is our Mediator between God and man. The tabernacle door represents Christ as the believer's only way to approach God.

B. The Pillars

There were five pillars for the door. Someone has said that these could well represent the five writers of the New Testament Epistles. This view is held perhaps because it is generally accepted that the four pillars for the gate are representative of the four writers of the Gospels.

The pillars at the door were made of shittim wood overlaid with gold and set into sockets of brass (Exod. 26:37). This was hardly the case of the pillars at the gate. We wish to think of the five (number of grace) pillars as representing our Lord. They were covered with gold, speaking to us again of His divinity; they were set over sockets of brass, speaking of His victory over our judgment which was placed upon Him. Judgment now is under His feet as it were, and He excels in all His power and glory.

We read in Isaiah 9:6 of five names given to the Lord Jesus: "Wonderful, Counselor, The Mighty God, The Everlasting Father, The Prince of Peace." Why just five? Did not the Holy Spirit reveal these to Isaiah as the Holy Spirit revealed to Bazaleel how the tabernacle should be constructed?

This message has an impact on Christian worship, but at the same time the simple story of salvation is found at every turn. The evangelistic appeal must not be overlooked. Only the Holy Spirit can direct a proper conclusion to these truths.

As we have mentioned before, frequent references to the illustrations, by focusing on the particular object under discussion, will contribute to the effectiveness of your study.

Outline 4

THE GOLDEN CANDLESTICK
(Exodus 25:31-40; 27:20, 21)

I.   MATERIAL: BEATEN GOLD—90 TALENTS (no size given)
   - A.   The Shaft ("I am the vine, ye are the branches," John 15:5)
   - B.   The Branches ("Ye are the light of the world," Matt. 5:14)

II.   THE SEVEN LAMPS

III.   THE OIL FOR THE LAMPS
   - A.   Made From Beaten Olive Oil
   - B.   The Only Light (no natural light)

The golden candlestick was a very important item within the tabernacle's holy place. Like all the other furniture, it was also very costly. At the end of each branch, and at the end of the central shaft, were lamps that contained the oil. The branches and the shaft were beaten into a series of knobs, bowls, and flowers. An equal number of these constituted each branch and the shaft.

I.   MATERIAL: BEATEN GOLD—90 TALENTS (no size given)

Here again, we have gold representing the divinity of our Lord Jesus Christ. We do not have mere gold, but a beaten gold that had endured punishment. Of our Savior we read: "It pleased the Lord to bruise him," and again, "He was bruised for our iniquities" (Isa. 53:5, 10). God allowed this for Jesus in order to bring the Church into existence. It cost God infinite suffering to bring about the birth of the bride of Christ—the Church. Surely we are reminded, along with the apostle Peter: "Unto you, therefore, which believe he is precious . . ." (1 Peter 2:7).

The weight of the candlestick was 90 talents, which represents approximately $30,000 in value (based on established values during the time the United States was on the gold standard). Ninety Hebrew talents represents approximately 94 pounds (Webster). Other than the weight and the general appearance, we know nothing of the dimensional characteristics of the candlestick.

In view of this, we are compelled to say there are no limitations placed on our Lord: He is omnipotent, omnipresent, and omniscient. He not only is unlimited and unrestricted, but His value is fathomless. The Incarnate Word is immeasurable. He is all the fullness of the Godhead bodily and full of grace and truth. We are redeemed, not with silver and gold, but with the precious blood of Jesus (see 1 Peter 1:18-19).

A. The Shaft ("I am the vine, ye are the branches," John 15:5)

This portion of the candlestick is the central stem from which three branches on each side were attached. (See enlarged view shown on the drawing, p. 67.) Not only does the candlestick represent Christ, but in a beautiful way the shaft specifically gives to us a picture of His relationship to His bride—the Church. Jesus said: "I am the vine, ye are the branches" (John 15:5). In the candlestick we have the shaft from which the branches protrude.

In Revelation 1:12, 13 we read: "I saw seven golden candlesticks; and in the midst of the seven candlesticks one like unto the Son of man." We have here, in the center of the seven golden candlesticks, one like Jesus. Jesus is called "Son of man" 26 times in the Gospel of Luke.

B. The Branches ("Ye are the light of the world," Matt. 5:14).

We have already alluded to the typological teaching found in the branches. We have seen, in a general sense, how the candlestick gives us a portrait of our Lord. As we focus our spiritual lens more clearly, we again see a picture of the believer—the bride of Christ. The candlestick branches were an integral part of the central shaft, so we become one in Christ and in due time shall be like Him.

We are called the bride of Christ. When a marriage takes place God sees two becoming one flesh. Spiritually, Christ and His Bride become one when we become married to our beloved Savior. Jesus said, "Ye are the light of the world." As long as Christ was in the world He was the light of the world, and He is still the light of the world but not in a fleshly body. He needs individuals, you and me, to shine forth His light in this dark, sinful world.

Jesus said: "Ye are the salt of the earth" (Matt. 5:13), and admonishes us to "let your light so shine before men, that they may see your good works, and glorify your Father which is in heaven" (Matt. 5:16).

Remember that the seven golden candlesticks in Revelation 1:20 are the seven churches mentioned immediately thereafter. These churches represent the gospel light shining down through this dispensation of grace. We believe it consistent with scriptural typology to see, in the seven lamps of the tabernacle candlestick, a shadow of the Church of Jesus Christ today giving forth the blessed light of the gospel message.

II. THE SEVEN LAMPS

In Revelation 4:5 we read of the "seven lamps of fire . . . which are the seven Spirits of God." Certainly there is no spiritual light in the world today except as the Holy Spirit sets on fire, as it were, the children of God. Our efforts to be a witness for Christ are useless except as the Holy Spirit motivates and directs us.

Seven, in the Word of God, often symbolizes divine perfection. Where can we find any more significance attached to this number than in the seven lamps representing God the Holy Spirit indwelling the Church of Jesus Christ?

III. THE OIL FOR THE LAMPS

We believe the oil for the lamps speaks to us of the Holy Spirit. Several times we find oil, in the Scriptures, used as a type of the Holy Spirit. Certainly showing forth light to the world today, as well as the proclamation of the Gospel, would be ineffective except for the work of the Holy Spirit. The candlestick would have been useless without the oil for the lamps.

Let us notice a few reasons why we believe this oil to be a type of the Holy Spirit. In Hebrews 1:9 we read: ". . . thy God, hath anointed thee with the oil of gladness above thy fellows." According to the text, God the Father is speaking to the Son. The gladness enjoyed by the Son would have been none other than the Person of the Holy Spirit operative in God the Son.

We are all familiar with the parable of the ten virgins (Matt. 25:1-13). A careful analysis of this parable tells us of those who could, and those who could not, enter into the marriage. The five foolish virgins were unable to enter because they did not possess oil. And just as the five foolish virgins were unable to approach the bridegroom, so humankind can not come to Christ, "except the Father draw him" (John 6:44). "If any man have not the Spirit of Christ, he is none of his" (Rom. 8:9).

Salvation cannot come to any individual without the supernatural working of the Holy Spirit upon the heart of that individual. It was the Holy Spirit hovering over the face of the waters and the spoken Word of God that brought light to this world (Gen. 1:2, 3). It was this same Holy Spirit who hovered over Mary and caused her to conceive and bring forth a Son, and brought Jesus, the Light of the world, into this sin-cursed world (Luke 1:35).

We find the oil for the lamps in the Book of Exodus

mentioned immediately after the outer court gate. This, we believe, illustrates for us the Holy Spirit active in the believer after the believer has come for salvation by God's appointed way.

A. Made From Beaten Olive Oil

Just as the candlestick was made of beaten gold, so the oil was made from the beaten olive. We believe this represents the sufferings of the Holy Spirit. We must always remember that the Holy Spirit is a Person, who has the sense of feeling even as you and I. "Grieve not the Holy Spirit of God" (Eph. 4:30). How it must have hurt the very heart of God to permit His Son to suffer the agony of Calvary for you and me. The olive was beaten, not just crushed, in order that the lamps might have oil and give forth their light.

B. The Only Light

The only light in the tabernacle was that radiating from the candlestick—no windows in the walls, no light carried by the priest while he daily performed his sacred duties in this holy place of worship. Jesus said: "I am the light of the world . . ." (John 1:9; 8:12), and we cannot approach God in worship except through Jesus Christ, the Light of the world.

The priest could not have carried on his sacred duties of worship without light with which to see. The candlestick provided that light. Jesus said: "No man cometh unto the Father, but by me" (John 14:6). When you and I worship God and petition Him, we must come by the way of His Son, the Light of the world; otherwise our prayers are worthless and our worship sheer mockery. We find the total absence of natural light in the tabernacle. Only the supernatural light of the glorious gospel of Christ can illuminate our hearts and minds and prepare us for eternity. Education, culture, or wealth found in this natural world will never suffice.

This message exalts the Lord Jesus Christ as the Light of the world in perfect cooperation with the Holy Spirit as the Chief Executor. You will want to investigate this further and elaborate on the complete gospel message.

Outline 5

THE ALTAR OF INCENSE
(Exodus 30:1-10; Psalm 141:2;
Revelation 8:3, 4)

 I. MATERIAL AND SIZE
   A. Wood and Gold: 1 $1/_2$ feet by 1 $1/_2$ feet by 3 feet
       high
   B. The Horns
   C. The Crown
 II. RELATIVE POSITION
 III. THE ALTAR FIRE

You will see from the Scripture reading in the Psalms and
the Revelation how this altar typifies prayer or worship. This
altar was a small piece of furniture, but sufficiently large to
serve its purpose. It is not the large or long prayer that avails
much, but the prayer of faith. We are not heard for our vain
repetitions, but the "fervent prayer of a righteous man availeth
much" (James 5:16). The golden altar of incense is a type of
Christ in respect to the efficacy of His mediatorial work for us
(Heb. 7:25; 8:1).

I. MATERIAL AND SIZE

A. The Wood Overlaid With Gold: 1 $1/_2$ feet by 1 $1/_2$ feet by 3 feet high

As in each case previously, this material speaks of the
humanity in our Lord enhanced by His divinity or deity. If the
size has any particular significance, we cannot ascertain what

that significance may be. Perhaps the fact that this altar was foursquare, as was the brazen altar, is meaningful.

B. The Horns

These were at the four corners of the altar, similar to those which we found on the brazen altar. The horns were also wood overlaid with gold. We found the horns on the brazen altar speaking to us of "power in the blood;" similarly, the horns on this golden altar speak to us of "power in prayer."

In addition to what we have stated in our outline on the brazen altar, we should like to emphasize the typical truth relevant to these horns. In 2 Samuel 22:3 we hear David singing about the horn of salvation. The gospel is the power of God unto salvation. We see how this refers to Jesus Christ, who is our salvation.

Why wood and gold? Why any horns on the altar at all? They apparently served no useful purpose, except to complete the type and beautiful picture that we have of Jesus Christ. How wonderful are His ways, and past finding out. Christ, the creator of the universe (Col.1:16), is the horn or power of our salvation, and we are kept by His absolute omnipotence (1 Peter 1:5).

These horns were sprinkled with blood from the brazen altar once a year on the day of atonement. God never forgets the suffering His Son endured for us. We must never forget the efficacy of the blood of Christ.

In the Gospel of Luke we read: God "hath raised up a horn of salvation for us in the house of his servant David" (1:69). It was Zacharias, father of John the Baptist, as he was filled with the Holy Spirit, who made this prophecy. Zacharias was a priest of God, and familiar with the altar of incense. The Holy Spirit undoubtedly directed him to use this terminology as he prophesied of Christ.

C. The Crown

We are all acquainted with the generally accepted meaning of a crown. The crown always speaks of exaltation. A golden crown was placed around the top of the altar of incense. This gives us a picture of Christ exalted. It is only because Christ was resurrected and exalted to the right hand of the Father that we can expect to realize the power of answered prayer (Heb. 9:24).

II. RELATIVE POSITION

The location of the altar relative to its surroundings is important (Exod. 40:5). In Revelation 8:3 we see a golden altar of incense placed before the throne. The altar in the tabernacle was also placed before the throne. We shall find, as we discuss the mercy seat, that it was the place of God's presence (Exod. 25:22), and that a crown of gold encompassed the ark upon which the mercy seat rested.

Today our great High Priest, the Lord Jesus, is not seated upon a throne, but before the throne at the right hand of God. It is because of His position before the Father that we have such a High Priest who can make perfect intercession for us (Heb. 7:25). And even beyond this, the "Holy Spirit also maketh intercession for us with groanings which cannot be uttered" (Rom. 8:26).

The altar of incense was placed according to divine plan just before the place of God's habitation. Our prayers are channeled directly to the Father through Jesus Christ, who resides according to divine plan before the throne of God.

There is one vast difference between the picture we have of the altar in the tabernacle and that in heaven today. In the tabernacle we find a barrier—the veil. The veil extended across the tabernacle and separated the Holy Place from the Most Holy Place. At the crucifixion, this veil was rent in two from the top to the bottom (see Outline Seven). We now have direct access to the throne of God because of Christ's finished work.

Israel could never approach the Most Holy Place in the tabernacle. The high priest could enter this place only once a year, and then only if he had applied the blood to atone for his own sins. How we praise God for His unspeakable gift, Jesus

Christ our Savior, who has opened the way to the throne of grace!

III. THE ALTAR FIRE

This fire was taken from off the brazen altar found in the outer court. We have seen how the fire on the brazen altar, to which the sacrificial lamb was subjected, represents the fiery judgment of God against His Lamb. We know that because Christ endured this suffering for us, we receive His salvation. As the fire for the brazen altar was effective, so our prayer, or intercession, is effective today only because of Christ's finished work on the cross.

We are prone to think only of Christ dying for our sins. He did this, for which we praise God, but His death and resurrection did so much more than that for us. We may now enjoy, and submit by direct communication, our personal petitions to God the Father. We can realize the effects, in this life, of Christ's intercessory work and the hope of being with Him throughout eternity. In addition to this, we have for ourselves many other precious promises which are given to us in His Word.

This message centers around the general theme of prayer. Almost any other available material on the subject of prayer would be helpful to your study. I would also suggest a review of the material in Outline One.

Outline 6

THE TABLE OF SHEWBREAD
(Exodus 25:23-30; Leviticus 24:5-9; Matthew 12:3, 4; John 6:33-35)

I. MATERIAL AND SIZE: WOOD AND GOLD 1 $^1/_2$ feet by
   2 $^1/_2$ feet high by 3 feet long
   A. Typical Significance: Fellowship
   B. The Crowns
   C. The Border
II. THE UNLEAVENED BREAD (12 loaves)
   A. Made From Fine Flour
   B. Made Without Leaven

"Behold, I stand at the door, and knock: if any man hear my voice, and open the door, I will come in to him, and *will sup with him, and he with me"* (Rev. 3:20). Here we have the Lord Jesus speaking concerning the conditions by which we have fellowship with Him; namely, open the door of your heart. How many times during our Lord's earthly ministry do we see Him at a table with those whom He loved! Our Lord yearns to have that same sweet fellowship and communion with you and me today. He is the Bread of Life (John 6:32-35). The invitation is "Come and dine." Here in the tabernacle we have the table set before us.

I. MATERIAL AND SIZE: WOOD AND GOLD (1 $^1/_2$ feet by 2 $^1/_2$ feet high by 3 feet long)

We see in the material once again the humanity and divinity of Christ—One born of a woman, born of the flesh, the incarnate Son of God; the wood and the gold typifying again this twofold aspect of our Lord.

The priest could not sit at the table of shewbread. It was too small, sufficiently large only to support the 12 loaves. Even if he could have sat at this table, there were no chairs or other provisions for rest in the tabernacle. The priests were always standing as they administered their duties.

We turn to Hebrews 10:11, 12: "And every priest standeth daily ministering and offering oftentimes the same sacrifices, which can never take away sin: But this man [Christ], after he had offered one sacrifice for sins forever, *sat down* on the right hand of God."

There is no rest for the human soul except as we trust in the finished work of our great High Priest, who is seated at the right hand of God and making intercession for us. He finished His work and can therefore rightfully sit in His place in glory.

We attach no special significance to the size of this table. Dimensions imply limitations. While the gospel is to "whosoever will," only those who place their trust in the Bread of Life can enjoy fellowship around this table. In other words, fellowship around this table is limited to believers only.

A. Typical Significance: Fellowship

We are all familiar with Psalm 23:5: "Thou preparest a table before me in the presence of mine enemies." As we mentioned in the beginning, the Lord yearns for our fellowship around the table that He has prepared. We are reminded of the Lord's Supper and how we are expected to remember His death around His table. The table of shewbread speaks symbolically of communion and fellowship with the Bread of Life.

B. The Crowns

These were attached to the table top and they surrounded the loaves of shewbread. The unleavened shewbread speaks of the sinless Son of God—the Bread of Life. The crowns may well represent the exaltation of Christ.

There were two crowns. Perhaps these represent our twice-crowned Lord. He was crowned once with thorns, and the day is coming when He will be crowned King of Kings and Lord of Lords.

C. The Border

The border surrounded the loaves of shewbread and measured approximately 4 $\frac{1}{2}$ inches wide. We cannot clearly ascertain the purpose for this border. It may have functioned to prevent the loaves from falling off the table of shewbread. It appears more likely that the border provided a place for the utensils. In any event, its purpose was secondary to the table proper.

The border about this table at least illustrates for us the many helps available for use in the study of God's Word. Commentaries, concordances, and study courses surely are real helps for Bible study. As the border was closely related to the shewbread and served its purpose, so our commentaries, etc., are closely related to the Word of God and serve real purpose today. We shall see shortly how the shewbread represents for us not only our Lord as the Bread of Life, but also the Word of God.

II. THE UNLEAVENED BREAD (12 loaves)

There is one thing certain in respect to the typology here—whatever this bread was intended to represent, that something or someone must have been perfect.

We find this to be true because this bread must not contain any leaven or yeast. Now leaven in the Scriptures is always a type of sin. The following are a few passages which teach us this truth, either by inference or by direct statement: Exodus 12:15; Leviticus 2:11; Matthew 16:6; Mark 8:15; and 1 Corinthians 5:6-8.

We sincerely believe the unleavened bread speaks to us concerning both the living Word of God (Christ, who said, "I am the bread of life" John 6:35), and the written Word—our Bible. Concerning the living Word, the Lord Jesus, we read:

"For he hath made him to be sin for us, who knew no sin; that we might be made the righteousness of God in him" (2 Cor. 5:21). A life without leaven—the sinlessness of the Son of God!

The written Word was given to us by Israel. Twelve separate tribes constituted the nation Israel. The living Word (John 1:14), the Lord Jesus, chose 12 disciples, some of whom wrote a large portion of the New Testament. There were just 12 loaves of unleavened bread on the table of shewbread. The word "shewbread" means literally "presence bread," perhaps so named because of close proximity to the very presence of God in the tabernacle.

A. Made From Fine Flour

The Word of God states that this bread was made from fine flour. This is again a picture of Christ the living Word. There was nothing coarse or undesirable about this flour. There were other ones besides Pontius Pilate who said, "I find no fault in this man."

Flour, in itself, is anything but palatable. It must be subjected to the fire before it can be partaken of and appreciated. The wheat for the flour must be crushed before it can become usable as bread (Isa. 53:4). Our Lord's good life is not enough; He had to suffer the agony of the cross before you and I could be partakers of His grace. It is not His good example, and our efforts to follow that example, that saves our souls, but simple faith in His finished work on the cross.

B. Made Without Leaven

We have already touched on the typical significance here. Suffice it to say that the unleavened aspect of this bread is probably the most significant. I would suggest that the Scripture references already given in the first section of this Outline be studied carefully.

The priests' relationship to the shewbread was that it became their food. Is there not a lesson for us here? The priests, regardless of their dignity, self-righteousness, or elected position, were required to partake of the unleavened bread. It does not matter how good we may think we are, we too must take Christ, the living Word, into our hearts for salvation. His righteousness imputed to us, or charged to our account, is the only kind of righteousness God will recognize in that day. (Rom. 4:6; 9:30; 1 Cor. 1:30; 2 Cor. 5:21; Phil. 3:9).

The central theme of this message is "Christ, the Bread of Life." The gospel message can be most vividly and illustratively portrayed. There is room for elaboration in this message without becoming speculative in respect to the types.

Much of the success of this study will be predicated upon a proper conclusion. As always, we must rely upon the Holy Spirit for an effective personal application.

Outline 7

THE INNER VEIL
(Exodus 26:31-35; Matthew 27:50, 51;
Hebrews 10:20, 21)

   I.   THE UNRENT VEIL
       A. Its Place in the Tabernacle
       B. Physical Characteristics: Material, Colors,
            Cherubim
       C. The Pillars
  II. THE RENT VEIL
       A. Its Symbolical Meaning (type of Christ's death)
       B. Its Real Significance
           1. Man has access to the throne of God
           2. God's invitation to come

This subject should stir our hearts, perhaps as none other. We have before us a beautiful, sacred, and heart-searching picture. The inner veil was not just another veil or curtain. It was the innermost veil, with special significance and of utmost importance.

I. THE UNRENT VEIL

We wish to bring to your attention, first, the unrent veil — the veil as it appeared intact, not only in the tabernacle but later in the temple itself. This inner veil is a type of our Lord's human body. The Word of God is very specific in respect to the typology here. You have already read concerning this in Hebrews 10:20, 21: "Through the veil, that is to say, his flesh." With this truth in mind, we now see the unrent veil as representing our Lord before His crucifixion.

We see this veil in the tabernacle as a barrier to the priests who daily ministered in the Holy Place. The high priest could not enter into the Holy of Holies behind the veil in God's presence, except on one day a year. The one single thing preventing admittance to this most Holy Place was the unrent inner veil.

This was true until Christ came in the flesh and finished His work. Before His death and resurrection, humankind was unable to approach an infinitely holy God except through the mediatorial work of a God-appointed priest. Now, in this age of grace, we have access to the throne of God because the body of our Lord was rent on the cross, and because He arose victorious and now lives forever to make intercession for us.

A. Its Place in the Tabernacle

The inner veil separated the Holy of Holies place from the Holy Place. You will recall the Holy Place as that area 15 feet wide by 30 feet long which contained the candlestick, the altar of incense, and the table of shewbread. This was indeed a Holy Place, since this was God's appointed place of worship.

Materialistically speaking, God does not reside in holy places today. The Holy Spirit is dwelling now in many tabernacles. These are not tabernacles made with hands. The most holy and most sacred place on earth today is still where God the Holy Spirit dwells.

Where are these tabernacles wherein the Holy Spirit abides today? Again, let us turn to the Word of God. We read in 1 Corinthians 3:16, 17: "Know ye not that *ye* are the temple [or tabernacle] of God, and that the Spirit of God dwelleth in *you?* If any man defile the temple of God, him shall God destroy; for the temple of God is *holy, which temple ye are."* God is very jealous of His rightful place in your heart. To Him your heart is a sacred and holy place of communion and fellowship.

Listen further to His Word: "What? know ye not that your body is the *temple* of the Holy Spirit which is in you, which ye have of God, and ye are not your own?" (1 Cor. 6:19). The Holy Spirit is in the world today in bodily form, but the body He uses for a dwelling place is your body and mine. May we keep our bodies a fit place for Him to maintain His Holy presence!

Because God *does* have a place on earth in which to dwell—these fleshly bodies of ours—we are commanded to give our bodies to God as a present, which is a reasonable thing for us to do (see Rom. 12:1). This profound truth is reiterated in 2 Corinthians 6:16 and found to be a divinely established fact throughout the New Testament.

A divine perspective on whose property we are is the first step toward a happy and victorious Christian life. We have been bought with a price—the precious blood of Jesus.

The inner veil served as a veil in the sense that it covered or veiled the Holy of Holies place. The Holy of Holies is a picture of heaven and the throne of God, where God the Father dwells. Today the veil is rent, and we can know something of what heaven is like. We read much about heaven in the last Book of the Bible, but more than that, we are able to approach the throne of God. Some day when we see Him face to face we will fully realize this precious truth.

The veil prevented the priest from approaching the throne of God. The Israelites were never permitted to approach the Holy of Holies. Thank God, the believer today not only can approach the throne of God, but God has extended to him His invitation to come boldly to that throne. We will see this later as we discuss the rent veil.

B. Physical Characteristics: Material, Colors, Cherubim

Jewish tradition tells us that this veil, woven of pure Egyptian linen, was 4 inches thick. Interwoven within this veil were the characteristic colors—blue, purple, and scarlet. Also intrinsically woven into the veil were the cherubim. All of this speaks symbolically of Christ and the holiness of God, such as we found concerning the linen hanging for the tabernacle door, and the linen inner curtain that served as a ceiling for the tabernacle.

C. The Pillars

These were four in number and made from shittim wood overlaid with pure gold. These pillars differ in four ways from those at the court gate. They were twice as long, founded upon silver, covered with gold instead of brass, and were cut off at the top. We believe the veil pillars speak to us of the Christ of the Gospels. Just as these pillars were cut off, so His life was "cut off out of the land of the living" (Isa. 53:8). The material from which these pillars were made again speaks of both His humanity and deity, symbolized by the wood and the gold.

II. THE RENT VEIL

"And, behold, the vail of the temple was rent in twain from the top to the bottom; and the earth did quake, and the rocks rent" (Matt. 27:51). We have already discussed the precise statement in God's Word relevant to the veil as representative of the body of Christ (Heb. 10:20).

A. Its Symbolical Meaning

In Matthew's Gospel we have the account of this veil being completely torn apart from the top to the bottom, representing therefore His flesh torn on Calvary. We sincerely believe His cross was placed into a hole in the ground and His precious body hung suspended on cruel nails, according to the vivid account given to us in the Gospels, and the custom practiced by the Roman government at that time.

B. Its Real Significance

In John 10 we find repeatedly the statement by our Savior, "I lay down my life." As was the custom, Jesus laid Himself upon the cross while the cross lay upon the ground. This He did willingly as the nails were driven through His hands and feet. Then, while in spiritual, mental, and physical agony, the soldiers lifted that cross and secured it in a near perpendicular position—the infinite Son of God now dying to settle the sin question once for all.

The veil, that is to say His flesh, was completely rent. Our Lord's work on the cross is a completed work; Jesus said, "It is finished" (John 19:30).

1. Man Has Access to the Throne of God

What does all this mean to you and me? Besides providing a perfect and complete salvation, it means—unlike the priests of old—you and I can have immediate access to the throne of God. The way is now made open to God's throne through Christ's finished work.

2. God's Invitation to Come

We now have a special invitation to "come boldly unto the throne of grace, that we may obtain mercy, and find grace to help in time of need" (Heb. 4:16; see also Heb. 10:19-22). "That we may obtain mercy" is the salvation aspect of His invitation. "Find grace to help in time of need" is the burden-bearer aspect of God's invitation freely offered to the believer.

In addition, as if all this were not enough, the believer also has, as a result of the rent veil, the benefit of Christ's mediatorial work and the promise of an eternal dwelling place with our blessed Lord (Rom. 8:34; Heb. 7:25; John 14:2, 3).

Outline 8

ARK OF THE COVENANT
(Exodus 25:10-22; Hebrews 9:4)

    I.   PHYSICAL CHARACTERISTICS: SIZE AND MATERIAL
   II.   CONTENTS
         A. Tablets of the Law
         B. Golden Pot of Manna
         C. Aaron's Rod That Budded
 III.   RELATIVE POSITION
         A. In the Tabernacle
         B. On Journey

    The importance placed by Israel upon the ark of the covenant is astounding. The importance given to this ark by Jehovah God was stupendous. In respect to a study of its typical significance, these facts must be realized.

    There are three arks in the Bible: Noah's ark, the ark of Moses, and the ark of the covenant. Without exception each one speaks to us of preservation, and each in its own particular way portrays the Lord Jesus—our ark of refuge. One of the articles within the ark of the covenant was God's precepts—the Law. Just as the ark of the covenant encompassed, or shall we say preserved, God's precepts to Israel, so the Lord Jesus, as our everlasting covenant, has reserved for us the title deed to our salvation in heaven (Heb. 8:6; 13:20; 1 Peter 1:4).

I. PHYSICAL CHARACTERISTICS: SIZE AND MATERIAL

    While comparatively small, the ark nevertheless was a very valuable treasure chest. The ark was enhanced by a golden crown and covered with a pure beaten gold lid called the mercy seat. Integrally forged as a part of this mercy seat were two cherubim. The mercy seat will be considered in Outline Nine.

The ark was 3 feet 9 inches long, 2 feet 3 inches wide, and 2 feet 3 inches deep. A small piece of furniture, but how precious and sacred to Israel! The area immediately over the ark was hallowed by God's presence, for it was there He had said, "I will meet with thee" (Exod. 25:22).

As Israel journeyed about in the wilderness, only the ark was carried on the shoulders of the priests. Just as Christ has been exalted high and lifted up to the right hand of God, so the ark , when it was removed, was exalted above everyone or anything else. Just as the priests of Levi carried the ark high so all could see, so believers too should be as willing to exalt Christ and proclaim Him to the whole world. God had commanded that the ark should not be touched. Except for the grace of God you and I would have no right to reach out today and touch the Lord spiritually. Thank God, however, the invitation is "Come," and "Him that cometh to me I will in no wise cast out" (John 6:37).

The material of shittim wood overlaid with pure gold represents both the humanity and deity or divinity of Christ.

II. CONTENTS

The typical significance attached to the articles within the ark may seem somewhat speculative. The author does not necessarily agree with previous thinking in regard to the typical meaning here. We cannot be dogmatic concerning biblical typology unless the typical truth is clearly seen in God's Word, or at least definitely implied.

A. Tablets of the Law

We believe these represent the written Word of God. The Ten Commandments are a portion of God's Word. The divine Law of God is holy and sacred; therefore, it belonged in the

Most Holy Place. The written Word is precious, and endures forever; thus it was preserved in the ark.

Inasmuch as the ark in a general sense was a type of Christ the Living Word, it is logical that the written Word should be closely associated with the ark. It was the spoken Word of God that brought creation into existence. God said, "Let there be light" (Gen. 1:3), and things began to happen. Who was this God, the Creator of all things? None other than your Savior and mine. "For by him were all things created" (Col. 1:16).

B. Golden Pot of Manna

There is little doubt that the manna given to Israel by Jehovah God as they trekked though the wilderness is a type of the Lord Jesus. Jesus said, "Moses gave you not that bread from heaven; but my Father giveth you the true bread from heaven. For the bread of God is he which cometh down from heaven, and giveth life unto the world" (John 6:32, 33 see also John 6:32-58.)

We believe the manna within the golden pot remained fresh, even though the manna that God provided every morning for the children of Israel was unfit for food the following day. You will recall how God for this reason had commanded Israel to gather only sufficient manna each day to supply their daily requirement. Christ, the Bread of Life, is sufficient for our daily needs and He is also sufficient for our eternal need after death has claimed these mortal bodies. We do know our Lord's body never saw corruption. We believe the manna is a type of Him.

C. Aaron's Rod That Budded

Aaron's rod was simply a lifeless piece of wood. You will remember how this rod came to life and budded when 11 other rods remained dead and lifeless (see Num. 17). We have here nothing less than life coming forth from death. Surely this is a type of Christ's resurrection from among the dead.

What more can we say, except that Aaron's rod not only budded, but blossomed out and brought forth fruit—almonds. Jesus said: "I am the resurrection and the life: he that believeth in me, though he were dead, yet shall he live" (John 11:25). He is the firstfruits, then we who are His share in His life. Jesus said: "Because I live, ye shall live also" (John 14:19). This is a message in itself, an inexhaustible one. Thank God for an omnipotent living Lord and Savior!

III. RELATIVE POSITION

The ark located in the Holy of Holies is a type of Christ glorified and in heaven. He was both humanity and deity; therefore, we have One in heaven who was like mankind, except sinless. Because He is both man and God He can and does serve as our great High Priest before the throne of God.

A. In the Tabernacle

The ark was located just before the ark of incense; however, the veil stood as a barrier between the two. We have seen the significant truth associated with this altar, how the burning incense was a picture of the prayers of the saints ascending to God. Today our prayers are very close to the throne of God and without a barrier between. The fire for the altar of incense was taken off the brazen altar. Our prayers to God are effective only if that same spiritual fire that transformed our hearts when we received Christ still burns in our hearts today.

B. On Journey

When Joshua was about to conquer Canaan, God commanded the priests to carry the ark before the people (Josh. 3:3, 4). On other occasions the ark was in the midst of the people as they journeyed. Just as the ark was always where it was most needed, so Christ is more willing to help us in time of need than we are willing to be helped. He is more ready to lead us than we are to be led. He is a very present help in time of need. If we stumble, the fault is not His but our own. May God help us as we pray to really believe He answers prayer! May we come regularly to the Word of God in order that our faith may continually increase (Rom. 10:17).

Where is the ark of His covenant or testament today? Where are all these valuable and sacred tabernacle furnishings now? We only know they were carried away many years later into Babylon during the Captivity. There is one astounding statement, however, concerning the ark of His testament, found in the Book of the Revelation (Rev. 11:19). John saw the ark in heaven. Perhaps it is preposterous to conclude this to be the same ark; however, we know all things are possible with God. One thing for certain, the true Ark, Christ Jesus, is there.

The high priest was permitted to approach the ark only one day a year, providing he had properly applied the blood taken from the brazen altar; but Christ, who became our High Priest, is always present before the Father making intercession for you and me. God the Father is ever mindful of the once slain Lamb now seated at His right hand (Mark 16:19; Heb. 7:25).

The ark is no longer on journey. Jesus Christ is no longer on journey but waiting for the Father's command to once more leave His heavenly glory and return to receive His own unto Himself (John 14:3; Acts 1:11). When He comes, it will be with a shout and with power, contrasted with His first coming as the meek and lowly One born in Bethlehem.

This discussion, in addition to being evangelistic, should persuade all of us as Christians to take advantage of Christ's mediatorial work and confess our sins, believing 1 John 1:9 as we do so.

Outline 9

THE MERCY SEAT, CHERUBIM, AND SHEKINAH GLORY
(Exodus 25:17-22; Leviticus 16:2; Psalm 80:1)

I. THE MERCY SEAT
   A. A Meeting Place
   B. A Resting Place
   C. A Place of Mercy
   D. A Throne
II. CHERUBIM
   A. Their Purpose
   B. Their Attitude
III. SHEKINAH GLORY

The mercy seat and cherubim consisted of one integral unit made from solid beaten gold. Perhaps this speaks of His glory and deity being one. The only other article within the tabernacle similarly constructed was the candlestick.

In respect to the material here, we do not find the presence of wood. We do not find humanity represented in any way. There is today spiritually, and in a very real sense, a place of mercy. This place of mercy was conceived and wrought by God.

We will discover that the shekinah glory represents the very presence of God, and the cloud veiled His presence. This cloud led His people Israel, and the Holy Spirit similarly leads His people today.

I. THE MERCY SEAT

Permit us to analyze the word "mercy seat." There are two

words found in the New Testament that give to us essentially the basic meaning of this word. We find in 1 John 2:2, the word "propitiation:" "And he is the propitiation for our sins: and not for ours only, but also for the sins of the whole world." Again in Romans 3:25: "Whom God hath set forth to be a propitiation through faith in His blood, to declare his righteousness for the remission of sins that are past, through the forbearance of God." Bible scholars indicate the root meaning of the word "mercy seat" (as found in Heb. 9:5) to be the same word as "propitiation" (Greek *hilastērion*), found in Romans 3:25 and 1 John 2:2.

The mercy seat had to be sprinkled with blood in order to accomplish the work of atonement. According to the New Testament, Jesus Christ became our propitiatory sacrifice, our mercy seat, or place of mercy. God had said He would meet with His people over the mercy seat, and because of His redeeming blood, God has mercy for the sinner and can forgive to the uttermost. Sin is infinite in the eyes of an infinite God who is absolute holiness. Therefore, only the infinite Son of God could suffice as an acceptable sacrifice before God the Father.

Because, from God's point of view, sin is infinite, it follows that the penalty for sin must also be infinite and eternal (Rev. 20:10, 15). The infinite Son of God, because of who He was, suffered sufficiently to pay the price for every sin committed by the human race. Our finite minds are not able to grasp this profound truth. We must accept this wonderful, marvelous grace by faith, for how else could a sinner ever be saved? Thank God for His unspeakable gift!

A. A Meeting Place

The blood-sprinkled mercy seat was a place where sinful mankind could have a rendezvous with mercy. The blood of Jesus Christ and His very presence at the right hand of God is, through faith in His blood, our meeting place with mercy. His finished work and mediatorial work at the right hand of His majesty on high assures both the sinner and the saint of forgiveness for sin.

B. A Resting Place

We have seen the mercy seat as a type of Jesus Christ. Literally, a seat is a place for rest. Where else in this world today can we find rest for our souls? Certainly in this time-squandering, grasping for pleasure age, we need an anchor that is steadfast and sure. We need to find that haven of all resting places—Jesus Christ our Lord and Savior. Jesus said: "Come unto me, all ye that labor and are heavy laden, and I will give you rest. Take my yoke upon you, and learn of me; for I am meek and lowly in heart: and ye shall find rest unto your souls. For my yoke is easy, and my burden is light" (Matt. 11:28-30).

C. A Place of Mercy

Just as the name implies, the mercy seat was a place of mercy. Once a year the high priest entered this Most Holy Place and sprinkled the mercy seat with blood taken from the brazen altar. God saw this blood as representing that of His own Son and recognized this expression of faith. As a result, God was merciful to His people and to the high priest and postponed judgment for sin. This happened on the day known as the Day of Atonement (Lev. 16).

A literal translation of the word "atonement" could very well be "at-one-ment." This signifies a reconciliation between God and sinful man. The word "reconciliation" or "reconciled" is a New Testament word which has the same root meaning as the word "atonement" found in the Old Testament (Eph. 2:15-18; 2 Cor. 5;18, 19).

D. A Throne

A throne is universally accepted as a place of judgment and also at times a place of mercy. The mercy seat was a place where God met to judge the sins of His people. As He saw the blood sprinkled thereon He would pass judgment. He had said just before His people came out of Egypt: "When I see the blood, I will pass over you" (Exod. 12:13). In other words,

God suspended judgment for sin until His own Son would come and pay the debt once for all.

When Jesus came, He removed the sin debt: past, present, and future. Man's sin was covered until the One who was prophesied to come did come and remove the sin of His people. Now our sins are removed as far as the east is from the west, and they are cast into the deepest sea, never more to be remembered against us (Ps. 103:12; Jer. 31:34; Heb. 8:12; 10:17). Praise God! Our sin is no longer merely covered but completely removed.

The crown at the outer edge of the mercy seat did more than enhance. The crown speaks of Christ's exaltation, His royal highness of kingship. Jesus, although rejected by Israel, nevertheless was born King of the Jews and will one day be crowned King of Kings and Lord of Lords.

He is all this and more because of His glorious resurrection from among the dead. Jesus said: "Because I live, ye shall live also" (John 14:19). Real life in Christ begins here and now, not after death. The Apostle Paul said: "For to me to live [life] is Christ, and to die is gain" (Phil. 1:21). Paul is saying, "For me, *life* is Christ;" nothing else counted as far as Paul was concerned.

II. CHERUBIM

These overshadowed the mercy seat and looked down upon it. They were figures representing angelic beings.

A. Their Purpose

Their responsibility seems to be that of guarding the infinite holiness of God. We gather this from their purpose at the east entrance to the Garden of Eden after Adam and Eve had sinned. They had been placed at this entrance by God Himself to guard the tree of life (Gen. 3:24).

B. Their Attitude

They looked down upon the blood-sprinkled mercy seat and covered the mercy seat with their wings (Exod. 25:20).

Their posture indicated God's value placed on the blood-sprinkled mercy seat. God's value placed upon the blood of Jesus Christ is fathomless, the most precious object in all of heaven. In connection with this, we should make a special study of such Scriptures as: Acts 20:28; Rom. 5:8, 9; Eph. 1:7; 1 Peter 1:18, 19; and Rev. 12:7-12.

Our attitude toward Christ and His precious blood has been wonderfully expressed by the apostle Peter: "Forasmuch as ye know that ye were not redeemed with corruptible things, as silver and gold, from your vain conversation received by tradition from your fathers; but with the precious blood of Christ, as of a lamb without blemish and without spot" (1 Peter 1:18, 19). "Wherefore also it is contained in the scripture, Behold, I lay in Zion a chief cornerstone, elect, precious; and he that believeth on him shall not be confounded. Unto you, therefore, which believe he is precious . . ." (1 Peter 2:6, 7).

III. SHEKINAH GLORY

This is an untranslated Hebrew word meaning, "There will I meet with you." You will recall the shekinah glory as God's presence over the mercy seat. It was here God had said He would meet with His people; that is, over the blood which had been sprinkled thereon.

God does not meet with sinful man today except as He sees the blood of Jesus Christ. There is no approach, no mercy, or any salvation today except through a personal recognition of the efficacy of Christ's blood, and a personal exercise of simple faith in that blood. This is the basis of New Testament doctrine and there is no substitute for it. Any church that digresses or deviates from this truth has become apostate, and the wrath of God will fall upon it (John 3:36; 8:24; 1 Thess. 1:7-9).

This message should become the pivotal focus of your study on the tabernacle. Here is an opportunity to discover the grace of our Lord Jesus Christ and appropriate God's love for you, perhaps as never before.

Outline 10

THE HIGH PRIEST
(Exodus 28; Hebrews 7:24, 25; 8:1, 2;
1 John 2:1, 2)

I. THE EPHOD: COLORS AND MATERIAL—Gold, Blue, Purple, Scarlet, and White
II. THE CURIOUS GIRDLE OF THE EPHOD
III. THE ONYX STONES: the Engraved Names
IV. THE BREASTPLATE OF JUDGMENT
    A. The Precious Stones
    B. Urim and Thummim
V. THE ROBE
VI. THE GOLDEN PLATE
VII. THE COAT
VIII. THE MITER

In the beginning man acted as his own high priest. We remember Cain and Abel offering their sacrifices to God. Later we find the father, as head of the household, offering sacrifices to God. Abraham was one of many who practiced this sacred duty. Still later in the history of mankind, we find a man chosen of God to act as priest for a nation, and finally Christ Himself as priest for the entire world. Jesus said: "No man cometh unto the father, but by me" (John 14:6).

The priest of which we are particularly concerned is God's chosen man Aaron, brother of Moses. Aaron was commissioned by Jehovah God to serve as High Priest for Israel. He not only was called (Exod. 28:1; Heb. 5:4, 10), but he was cleansed in order to be properly prepared to perform his sacred duties (Exod. 29:4).

The believer today is acting as a priest for the unsaved. The believer's prayer of intercession on behalf of the lost is certainly his sacred duty and a responsibility commensurate with or greater than that of any former earthly priest. The Bible identifies the Christian as one who is a priest (Rev. 1:6).

As Aaron was called of God and cleansed, so the believer in Christ has been called and cleansed (2 Thess. 2:13; 14; John 15:3). Aaron, the high priest of Israel, was immaculately clothed and wonderfully consecrated (Exod. 29:5, 6, 9). Even so, we as believers in Christ are clothed with His righteousness and consecrated by God for His service (Isa. 61:10; 2 Tim. 2:21). The word "consecration" is almost synonymous with the word "sanctification." This is something God does for us. We may dedicate our lives to Christ, but only God Himself can do the consecrating or sanctifying.

Now let us see Aaron as a type of Jesus Christ, our High Priest today. There are many references to this in the Bible, particularly in the Book to the Hebrews, beginning with chapter 3. While Christ is a priest after the order of Melchizedek, He executes His office after the pattern of Moses. In Hebrews 7 we have the order given, while Hebrews 9 reveals the pattern. Aaron's high priestly work was only a shadow of what Christ came to do and can do now for you and me. "Wherefore he is able to save them to the uttermost that come unto God by him, seeing he ever liveth to make intercession for them" (Heb. 7:25).

Aaron was both a compassionate and a commissioned high priest (Heb. 5:1, 2; Lev. 8). Jesus Christ also is both of these and more too. How many times have we read, "and he was moved with compassion"? (also Heb. 2:17). Christ was commissioned by the Father to come to this world on our behalf (John 3:17). Christ has also commissioned the believer to go and preach the gospel to every creature and baptize all who believe in Him (Mark 16:15, 16).

I. THE EPHOD

The ephod was worn by Aaron and his successors as they

performed their priestly duties in the Holy Place. This was an outer garment of linen and gold. The gold, as in the tabernacle, may well represent the deity of Christ, and the linen His infinite righteousness. The colors, we believe, speak of Christ in the same significant way we have found them to represent Him throughout the tabernacle (see Outline One, "The Gate").

In addition to the typical truth already given, it is interesting to know that the colors blue and red mingled together produce purple, which illustrates for us, if nothing else, divinity and humanity mingled together, producing King Emmanuel, the incarnate Son of God.

Concerning gold, which is typical of deity, it is interesting to know that gold is one metal that does not diminish in weight when subjected to intense heat; also, one ounce of gold may be extruded into a wire 500 feet long or into a leaf covering 56 square inches.

II. THE CURIOUS GIRDLE OF THE EPHOD

A girdle oftentimes denotes service or action. We gather this somewhat from the spiritual armor described for us in Ephesians 6:13-18. Here we are admonished, among other things, to gird ourselves about with truth, and to put on the whole armor of God, ready to do battle against the onslaughts of Satan.

The curious girdle appears to be an integral part of the ephod. We have seen the ephod as illustrative of Christ. The girdle, associated as it is with the ephod, could therefore represent Christ—ready as servant of mankind.

The original meaning of the word "curious" is "device." Perhaps a more descriptive name for the girdle would be a cunningly devised girdle.

III. THE ONYX STONES

These were placed on the shoulders of the priest. In each stone were engraved six of the names of the 12 tribes of Israel. Shoulders are for bearing burdens. The priests were to bear the burdens of the 12 tribes and these engraved stones were vivid reminders of this.

Christ, as our High Priest, is our burden bearer, and our names are written down also, not on His shoulders but in the Lamb's Book of Life.

The 12 names of the tribes of Israel were all engraved in the onyx stones, speaking perhaps of one common ground for salvation. The names were engraved in chronological order, according to their births (Exod. 28:10). Our names are written in the Lamb's Book of Life because of our rebirth (John 3:7), and perhaps in the same order as each one today comes to Christ for salvation.

IV. THE BREASTPLATE OF JUDGMENT

We are told that this name literally means "ornament of decisions." While we have in the Old Testament "the breastplate of judgment," in the New Testament we find "the breastplate of righteousness" (Eph. 6:14). The breastplate of judgment worn by the high priest was foresquare as was the brazen altar.

A. The Precious Stones

The breastplate of judgment displayed 12 precious stones set in pure gold, and placed uniformly in rows. Every stone was different, but they were set in only one breastplate. Each stone had the name of a tribe of Israel engraved upon it. Not only do we have here a picture of Israel, close to the heart of God, but the believer in Christ as well. Just as the precious stones were set in gold, so are we in Christ and placed there by God Himself (John 15:16). Just as there was one breastplate, but many jewels, so there is one Church, but many believers.

In the interest of brevity, we will describe each jewel specifically and subsequent related data pertinent to it. Along with each tribal name, some of its characteristics are listed:

Jewel	Tribe	Tribal Characteristics	
SARDIUS Predominantly red	JUDAH (Praise)	The tribe through which Christ came.	Red representing the blood sacrifice of Christ.
TOPAZ Brilliant yellow Topaz means "to seek"	ISSACHAR (Reward)	A cheerful people	The yellow may represent cheerfulness, having received a reward after diligently seeking.
CARBUNCLE A glittering jewel. Color unknown	ZEBULUM (Dwelling)	Served as a haven for ships (Gen. 49:13)	This tribe perhaps served the same purpose as harbor lights today.
EMERALD Sea Green	REUBEN (See a son)	Like the troubled sea: unstable, very sinful	
SAPPHIRE Second hardest known stone	SIMEON (Hearing)	Hard and ruthless	
DIAMOND Hardest of all stones	GAD (A troop)	Great warriors	1 Chronicles 5:18
LIGURE Characteristics obscure	EPHRAIM (Very fruitful)	Youngest son of Joseph	
AGATE Reflects its beauty only when split. A semi-translucent compound mineral	MANASSEH (Forgetting)	The tribe of Manasseh was divided.	Oldest son of Joseph
AMETHYST Purple	BENJAMIN (Son of may right hand)	The smallest tribe. A warring tribe.	Christ is the Son of the Father's right hand.
BERYL Meaning to break or subdue	DAN (Judge)	Led Israel into idolatry.	Judges 18:30, 31
ONYX Fire-like: very brilliant and very precious	ASHER (Blessed)	Genesis 49:20	
JASPER Clear as crystal. Sometimes bright yellow (Rev. 21:10, 11)	NAPHTALI (My wrestlings)	Freedom-loving	Genesis 49:21

The tribes of Joseph and Levi were not inscribed on the breastplate jewels or stones. Joseph was represented by his two sons—Manasseh and Ephraim. Joseph, which means fruitful, was born because God Himself had intervened (Gen. 30:22-24). He became a perfect type of Jesus Christ.

The name Levi means "joined closely." This tribe was sanctified, or set apart, to perform the holy rites associated with the tabernacle form of worship. Aaron, of course, was a member of the tribe of Levi, as was each succeeding priest of Israel.

B. Urim and Thummim

As far as can be ascertained, these words mean "lights and perfections." They too may have been precious stones. It appears that in some peculiar way these articles were used to assist in making important decisions. This we gather from 1 Samuel 28:6 and Numbers 27:21.

Perhaps the Urim and Thummim represent for us the Old and New Testaments. David said: "Thy word is . . . a light unto my path" (Ps. 119:105). David had only a portion of the Old Testament. Certainly the Pentateuch and the writings of the Prophets were a light to guide the human race during the Old Testament era.

The New Testament centers around the Perfect One—Christ Jesus. The New Testament is the Old Testament revealed. We have perfection here in the sense of perfection personified, who came to dwell among sinful men. Does not the Thummim, which means "perfections," illustrate the New Testament portion of the Word of God?

V. THE ROBE

This is the first time we find a Robe mentioned in the Scriptures. The Robe is a symbol of dignity (Ezek. 26:16), of royalty (Matt. 27:28, 29), and of righteousness (Isa. 61:10).

The Robe worn by the high priest was blue and had attached to its hem golden bells and pomegranates. The blue, as throughout the tabernacle, speaks, we believe, of the Divine Heavenly One, of whom the high priest was only a type. The pomegranates were blue, purple, and scarlet—the same significant colors found elsewhere, not only in the tabernacle but also upon the priest's outer garments. Perhaps the golden bells were worn to remind Israel that the one who intercedes for them was still alive and performing his divinely ordained work on their behalf. The believer today knows Christ is alive, if for no other reason because of the "joybells ringing in his heart."

On the Day of Atonement the bells were not worn; in fact, none of these beautiful garments were, but only a white garment. This was a day of humiliation—a picture of the sinner coming to Christ for salvation. Aaron, you recall, offered for his own sins also on this day. The joybells of salvation cannot ring until the sinner applies the precious blood of Christ to his heart and lets the Savior in.

VI. THE GOLDEN PLATE

This was worn about the head and consisted of pure gold. We have already emphasized the typical significance of gold, and the manner in which it represents Jesus Christ.

This gold plate or band was held in place in turn by a ribbon of blue. Inscribed upon the plate were the words, "Holiness to the Lord" (Exod. 28:36).

VII. THE COAT

It was of linen and skillfully embroidered. There is nothing ordinary about God's plans. The linen once again speaks of God's divinely imputed righteousness (Rev. 19:8; Isa. 61:10). The Scriptures tell us very distinctly that Christ is our righteousness (1 Cor. 1:30). The linen coat, therefore, pictures for us Jesus Christ.

This was an extraordinary coat. Some see in Jesus just an ordinary man—a great teacher, and full of good works, but the Bible says He is the Son of God (John 3:16).

VIII. THE MITER

It appears that only the high priest wore the miter while the other priests wore bonnets (Exod. 28:39, 40). Both were composed of fine linen, speaking symbolically of divine righteousness, as we have already observed.

The miter and the bonnets were coverings for the head. This in itself is a symbol of obedience to a higher order. Even in everyday life we find leadership requires a measure of righteousness. A person subject to intoxication, for example, could not continue to provide good leadership. Jesus Christ is our leader; more than that—our Good Shepherd and Savior. He is the perfectly righteous One and gives to us His righteousness in exchange for simple faith and trust in Him.

The message on the priesthood is a subject in itself and this outline is only a feeble attempt to cover some of the facets associated with this study. You may choose to divide this outline into several studies or rearrange the order from that given in the outline.

You will find within the main points of this outline the Lord Jesus Christ as the Human and Divine One, the Serving One, the Loving One, the Righteous One, and the Obedient One. The Word of God declares: "There is one God, and one mediator between God and men, the man Christ Jesus" (1 Tim. 2:5). Jesus Christ is our High Priest today and the only One who can perform the mediatorial work of a priest.

In the world about us we recognize that a man may mediate only for other persons. A man cannot mediate for a person and a member of the animal kingdom. Jesus Christ was both God and man and can, therefore, mediate for God and man. Man himself could never accomplish this, no matter what or who he may be.

SUMMARY

The best possible summary ever written on this inexhaustive subject is found in the Word of God—Hebrews, chapters 8, 9 and 10. We have made reference to portions of these chapters on numerous occasions. If you will not only read, but diligently study, these three chapters, the subject of the tabernacle in the wilderness will open up to you more readily.

Essentially, a brief bird's eye view of our subject matter should follow along this vein: We have, first of all, sinful man's approach to God for salvation and finding this salvation at the brazen altar, and that by simple faith in the shed blood of a lamb that was without spot or blemish. From this point, man came to the Word of God for daily cleansing and to satisfy his spiritual need. This is represented by the brazen laver. His next step is into the tabernacle proper, a place of divine worship, and finally to the most Holy Place beyond the veil, which is a symbol of heaven itself. Heaven is man's final resting place, contingent, of course, upon his receiving God's appointed way.

In these outlines we have attempted to explain clearly from the Word of God the only way of salvation. We trust that some will have been brought closer to their Lord while others will have received Christ as their personal Lord and Savior.

ILLUSTRATION OF THE FURNITURE

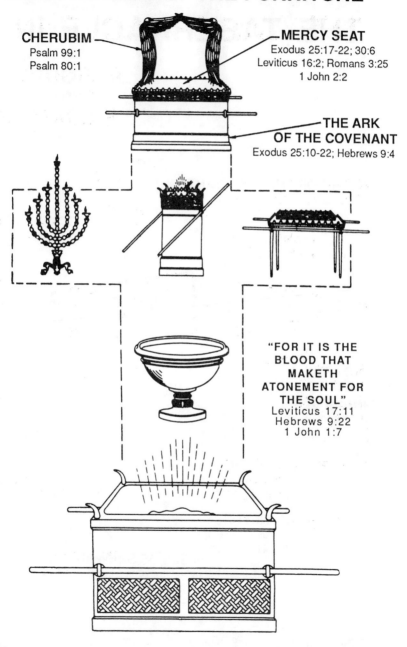

CHERUBIM
Psalm 99:1
Psalm 80:1

MERCY SEAT
Exodus 25:17-22; 30:6
Leviticus 16:2; Romans 3:25
1 John 2:2

**THE ARK
OF THE COVENANT**
Exodus 25:10-22; Hebrews 9:4

"FOR IT IS THE
BLOOD THAT
MAKETH
ATONEMENT FOR
THE SOUL"
Leviticus 17:11
Hebrews 9:22
1 John 1:7

THE TABERNACLE IN

A FIGURE
Hebrews 9:8, 9, 24

EXAMPLES
Hebrews 8:5

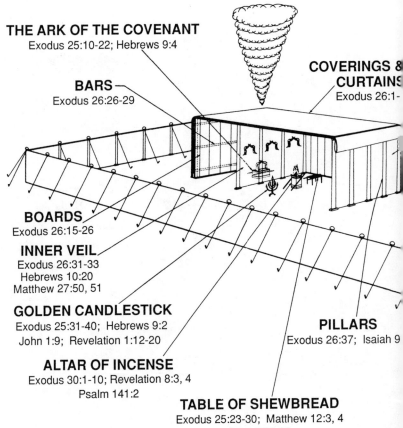

THE ARK OF THE COVENANT
Exodus 25:10-22; Hebrews 9:4

**COVERINGS &
CURTAINS**
Exodus 26:1-

BARS
Exodus 26:26-29

BOARDS
Exodus 26:15-26

INNER VEIL
Exodus 26:31-33
Hebrews 10:20
Matthew 27:50, 51

GOLDEN CANDLESTICK
Exodus 25:31-40; Hebrews 9:2
John 1:9; Revelation 1:12-20

PILLARS
Exodus 26:37; Isaiah 9

ALTAR OF INCENSE
Exodus 30:1-10; Revelation 8:3, 4
Psalm 141:2

TABLE OF SHEWBREAD
Exodus 25:23-30; Matthew 12:3, 4
John 6:33-35

THE WILDERNESS

A SHADOW
Hebrews 10:1

PATTERN
1 Corinthians 10:11

EAST

THE DOOR — Exodus 26:36, 37
"I AM THE DOOR" — John 10:7, 9

OUTER COURT
Exodus 27:9-15; Revelation 19:8

THE GATE — Exodus 27:16
"I AM THE WAY" — John 14:6; Acts 4:12

LAVER
Exodus 30:18-21; 38:8
John 15:3; James 1:23, 24

**BRAZEN ALTAR OF
BURNT OFFERING**
Exodus 27:1-8; John 1:29; Ephesians 5:2;
Hebrews 9:28; 10:12

THE HIGH PRIEST
Exodus 28:1; Hebrews 8:1, 2
7:24, 25; 1 John 2:12

GOLDEN PLATE
Exodus 28:36-38

ONYX STONES
Exodus 28:9-14

BREASTPLATE
Exodus 28:15-29
Ephesians 6:14

URIM & THUMMIM
Exodus 28:30
Numbers 27:21

COAT
Exodus 28:39
Revelation 19:8

CURIOUS GIRDLE
Exodus 28:8
Exodus 39:5
Luke 17:8
Isaiah 22:21

MITRE
Exodus 28:39

EPHOD
Exodus 28:6, 7

ROBE
Exodus 28:31-35
Isaiah 61:10
Job 29:14